A SWEAR A DAY

A DAILY DOSE OF RUDE
WORDS AND PROFANITIES

SID FINCH

A SWEAR A DAY

Copyright © Summersdale Publishers Ltd, 2023

Text by Rémy Dambron

An Hachette UK Company
www.hachette.co.uk

Summersdale Publishers Ltd
Part of Octopus Publishing Group Limited
Carmelite House
50 Victoria Embankment
LONDON
EC4Y 0DZ
UK

www.summersdale.com

Printed and bound in China

ISBN: 978-1-83799-012-2

Substantial discounts on bulk quantities of Summersdale books are available to corporations, professional associations and other organizations. For details contact general enquiries: telephone: +44 (0) 1243 771107 or email: enquiries@summersdale.com.

To:...

From:..

ARSE-CLOWN

N. A TOTAL BUFFOON, JOKESTER.
SOMEONE NOT TO BE TAKEN SERIOUSLY.

TOSSPOT

N. SOMEONE WHO INDULGES A
LITTLE TOO MUCH IN TOSSING BACK
A POT OF ALE. A DRUNKARD.

PETTIFOGGER

N. A LAWYER WHO EMPLOYS UNDERHANDED
AND UNSCRUPULOUS PRACTICES. A SHYSTER.

SEXORCISM

n. Stemming from the ideology that evil entities can exist within people who have been sexually deprived for an extended period of time, this ritual is basically indulging in some casual sex to release that demon. To sex someone happy, not just for their own benefit, but for the sake of others.

Example:
"Tom has been much more unhinged than usual this week. He completely lost his cool when I asked him about his date the other night. He could use a good sexorcism."

UP SHIT CREEK WITHOUT A PADDLE
EXPR. USED TO DESCRIBE BEING
STUCK IN A BAD OR UNFORTUNATE
SITUATION WITH NO CLEAR
SOLUTION OR WAY OUT.

SNOLLYGOSTER

n. Someone who will go to great
lengths to find themselves
holding power in public office,
often through lying and deceiving
their own constituents.

FERME TA GUEULE

expr. In French, "*gueule*" is used specifically to refer to an animal's mouth, here used as an even ruder way of saying "*shut your mug!*"

A HUEVO

expr. Although "*huevo*" means "*egg*" in Spanish, this short phrase is an interjection used to express enthusiastic agreement, such as "*right on!*" or "*fuck yeah!*"

TO BE BALLS DEEP

expr. To be so involved in a task or project that you can't take on a single thing more. To be extremely busy and stressed.

Example:

Brenda: *"Honey, can you pick up the kids this afternoon?"*
Ben: *"Sorry sweetheart, but there's no way! I'm still balls deep in paperwork and my weekly reports are due tomorrow!"*

NITWIT
n. An insult for a silly
or foolish person.

TO SHAG
v. To do the nasty, the
no-pants dance. To have sex.

CRAP ON A STICK
interj. Used to express surprise,
astonishment or disappointment.
Similar to "*shoot*" or "*dammit!*"

TO FUCK OVER

v. To treat someone so unfairly that it creates problems for them. To take advantage of someone in a way that makes their life much worse. To ruin them.

SARCHOTIC

adj. When someone is often so aggressively sarcastic that you can't tell if they are joking around or actually going bananas.

POS

N. STANDS FOR "*PIECE OF SHIT*",
SOMETHING THAT IS USELESS OR POORLY
MADE. IT CAN ALSO BE USED TO DESCRIBE
A PERSON WHO IS JUST AWFUL.

FUBAR

EXPR. STANDS FOR "*FUCKED UP
BEYOND ALL RECOGNITION*".

BFD

EXPR. STANDS FOR "*BIG FUCKING
DEAL*". IT IS USED SARCASTICALLY TO
MINIMIZE SOMETHING SOMEONE HAS
SAID OR DONE, AS IF IT MATTERS LITTLE
TO YOU OR THE REST OF THE WORLD.

BOLLOCKS

INTERJ. A NOUN THAT REFERS TO THE TESTICLES. IN ENGLAND IT IS ALSO USED AS AN INTERJECTION TO EXPRESS ANNOYANCE, DEFIANCE, DISGRUNTLEMENT OR THAT THE PERSON IS TALKING NONSENSE.

FUCKLING

n. Someone who is extraordinarily annoying and completely useless. It can also be used to describe the offspring of a couple who accidentally had a child as a result of careless unprotected sex.

SHIT-POUCH

n. Another word for one's mouth, particularly that of someone who talks a lot of shit.

DOUCHE-CANOE

n. A truly contemptible person. Someone quite unpalatable and obnoxious.

PECKERHEAD

n. Someone who is mean, unpleasant or lacks normal social skills.

TO KNOW FUCK ALL

expr. An insult to someone who is knowledgeably challenged. To not know much about anything or to not know anything about a particular subject.

Example:
"John knows fuck all about fine dining; why should we ask him which wine to pair with the salmon?"

TO RIP ARSE

V. A HEAVY-HANDED CUT OF THE OLD STINKY CHEESE. TO PASS GAS SO LOUDLY THAT IT SOUNDS LIKE THE WIND IS TEARING YOUR BUTT CHEEKS WIDE OPEN.

MILKSOP

N. A PERSON THAT IS WEAK AND LACKS COURAGE.

JERK

N. A RUDE AND HURTFUL PERSON WHO TAKES PLEASURE IN BEING UNLIKEABLE.

BULLSHIT ARTIST

n. Someone who is crafty, talented at deceiving others with words. Someone who masters pretending to know what they are talking about when they often don't have a clue.

ALL FART AND NO SHITE

expr. An Irish phrase describing someone who is full of big (and probably worthless) talk that is not backed up with action. Similar to "*all bark and no bite*".

SISSY

n. Someone who lacks courage, especially pertaining to situations that normally wouldn't require much bravery.

STICK IT WHERE THE SUN DON'T SHINE

expr. A fun way to tell someone off. A mild version of "*up yours!*"

CHODE

n. A short and stubby penis, but also used as an insult for someone who is a total dickhead.

SHUT YOUR PIE HOLE
EXPR. YOUR PIE HOLE IS YOUR
MOUTH. A MORE CREATIVE WAY
TO SAY *"SHUT YOUR MOUTH!"*

TO SHIT A BRICK
EXPR. TO BECOME EXTREMELY NERVOUS
OR FRIGHTENED ABOUT SOMETHING.

JABRONI
N. ITALIAN-AMERICAN SLANG FOR
SOMEONE WHO IS A WEIRDO OR
LOSER. A KIND OF KNUCKLEHEAD.

MOFO

N. SHORT FOR "*MOTHERFUCKER*", WHICH CAN BE USED AS AN INTERJECTION TO EXPRESS A VARIETY OF EMOTIONS RANGING FROM "*SON OF A BITCH!*" TO "*OUCH!*" THIS CAN ALSO BE USED AS A NOUN DESCRIBING SOMEONE WHO ACTS LIKE A REAL ARSEHOLE.

MALPARIDO

expr. One of the worst insults in Spanish you could throw at someone. Used throughout South America, it roughly translates to "*poorly given birth to*". In other words, someone who was "*fucked from the start*".

FERCOCKT
adj. Yiddish for "*FUBAR*"
(see page 11).

MADARCHOD
n. Hindi for "*motherfucker*".
A popular insult in India.

WANKER
n. Someone annoying, usually
male. From the verb "*wank*",
meaning to masturbate.

NO DUH

interj. A typically American impolite way of agreeing with something someone has said, as if it was common knowledge and didn't really need to be stated in the first place.

Example:
Fred: "*Ouch, this tea is hot!*"
Francine: "*No duh! You literally just watched me pour the water straight from the kettle!*"

HOT DAMN
INTERJ. WHEN YOU'RE
IMPRESSED OR SHOCKED, A SOFTER
ALTERNATIVE TO "*GODDAMN!*"

BLOW ME
EXPR. A VULGAR TAUNT THAT DOUBLES
AS AN INTERJECTION, USUALLY USED TO
EXPRESS INSOUCIANCE OR DISMISSAL.

SURE AS SHIT
EXPR. SIMILAR TO "*MOST DEFINITELY!*"
OR "*ABSOLUTELY!*" SOMETHING THAT IS
UNDENIABLY GOING TO HAPPEN. A SURE BET.

SHIT-EATING GRIN

expr. Describes a particularly evil-looking smile one wears when they know they've either done or are about to do something distasteful or sly. A very smug look.

PLAY A TUNE ON MY SKIN FLUTE

expr. A rude invitation for someone to perform oral sex on your penis. Can also be used as a colourful way of telling someone off after they've done something to upset you.

BAMPOT
n. Scottish for a foolish or obnoxious person.

CHESTICLES
n. A silly way of saying boobs or breasts. It can also refer to man boobs.

COCKAMAMIE
adj. Something implausible or ridiculous. It is usually an idea or plan that is unrealistic.

WHATEVER-THE-FUCK

expr. This phrase is often used in combination with other words to suggest a lack of understanding of something specific or of life in general, but in a way that one laments or wishes was different.

Example:

"I don't get what is so special about TikTok, but you know, with smartphones and social media, whatever-the-fuck these days..."

YUCK
INTERJ. AN EXPRESSION OF DISGUST,
ABOUT THE WAY SOMETHING EITHER
TASTES, LOOKS, SOUNDS OR FEELS.

SOURPUSS
N. SOMEONE WHO IS OFTEN
ILL-TEMPERED, POUTING OR IN A
CHRONICALLY BAD MOOD. A SULLEN PERSON.

BITCHY
ADJ. FROM THE NOUN "*BITCH*", THIS
DESCRIBES SOMEONE WHO IS HABITUALLY
DISAGREEABLE OR RUDE. TO HAVE AN
UNPLEASANT OR HOSTILE ATTITUDE.

BAGGER

N. A VULGAR INSULT FOR SOMEONE WHO IS SO UGLY THAT ANY OTHER REMOTELY INTERESTED PERSON WOULD HAVE TO CONSIDER PUTTING A BAG OVER THEIR FACE IN ORDER TO EVEN THINK ABOUT GETTING SEXUAL WITH THEM.

NOT PISSING ON SOMEONE WHEN THEY'RE ON FIRE

expr. Australian saying that basically means you care so little about someone that, even if they were on fire, you wouldn't pee on them to extinguish it.

ANKLE-BITERS

n. An unkind way of referring
to children, usually small
and annoying ones.

LIKE A DOG WITH TWO DICKS

expr. Refers to someone who is
sexually hyperactive, as dogs
are known to be rather horny.

MAGGOT

n. Popular term of belittlement in
the military. Refers to someone
who is inferior or despicable.

WTAF?

EXPR. STANDS FOR *"WHAT THE ACTUAL FUCK!?"* USED TO EXPRESS OUTRAGE OR PROFOUND CONFUSION, USUALLY IN AN ANGERED MANNER. A VARIATION ON WTF?

PISH

EXPR. A DATED INTERJECTION USED TO EXPRESS FRUSTRATION, ANNOYANCE OR DISGUST.

YOU GOTTA BE SHITTING ME

EXPR. SIMILAR TO *"YOU'RE JOKING, RIGHT?"* OR *"YOU MUST BE KIDDING"*, BUT A LOT HARSHER.

ABSO-FUCKING-LUTELY

adv. A stealthy way of inserting the
"*F*"-word into the middle of another
word. Used to emphatically agree
with something or someone. Quite
a few notches above "*hell yeah!*"

Example:
Vincent: "*Did you happen to catch
any of the last World Cup matches?*"
Laurent: "*Abso-fucking-lutely!
I watched almost every
one, it was magical!*"

SMELL-FEAST

n. An individual who has a particular knack for finding and getting invited to delicious feasts, almost like a parasite. The kind of mooch other guests tolerate out of politeness, but deep down they wonder how on earth this person fits into the group gathered around the table.

LITTLE SHIT

n. Someone devious or sneaky in a way that causes trouble for people around them. Also the kind of insult you yell at someone after they've successfully pranked you or made you look foolish.

MUMPSIMUS
n. Someone who is so stubborn that they deliberately make a mistake even though they have been shown it is wrong or false. Thickheaded to an embarrassing degree.

WALLOPER
n. Scottish for dick, both as an insult and as the actual phallus.

IGNORAMUS
adj. Someone who is not only purposefully ignorant but also a complete arsehole.

PANSY
N. A WEAKLING, A COWARD.

KNOB-DOBBER
N. SCOTTISH SLANG FOR A TOSSER
(SEE PAGE 53), A JERK.

TO BITCH ABOUT
V. TO COMPLAIN EXHAUSTIVELY ABOUT
SOMETHING AGGRAVATING TO YOU BUT OFTEN
WITHOUT THE SYMPATHY OF OTHERS.

PRAIRIE DOGGIN'

EXPR. TO BE "*YOYO-ING*" A TURD.
TO BE ON THE VERGE OF TAKING A SHIT, SO
MUCH SO THAT IT FEELS LIKE IT'S POKING ITS
HEAD IN AND OUT OF YOUR ANUS (MIMICKING
THE CLASSIC BEHAVIOUR OF A PRAIRIE DOG).

BEDGASM

n. The extreme pleasure one
experiences when entering the
freshly cleaned sheets of one's
bed. Feeling a sense of euphoria
to finally be crawling into bed,
especially after a long or tiring day.

BROWN-NOSER

n. A kiss-arse or bootlicker. Someone who flatters for personal gain. A suck-up.

SON OF A BISCUIT-EATER

n. In the southern US this is a less offensive way of saying *"son of a bitch!"*

DAGNABBIT

interj. In the southern US this is a mild version of *"damn it!"*

KAREN

n. A proper noun used as a pejorative term to describe an obnoxious, middle-aged, often racist person who acts in an aggressive and entitled manner in a very public way. What's more, this person is usually completely in the wrong, despite attempting to be perceived as some sort of victim. This term has gained particular notoriety in North America since 2020.

PUTAIN
INTERJ. FRENCH WORD FOR "*WHORE*",
MOST COMMONLY USED LIKE
"*GODDAMMIT!*" OR "*MOTHERFUCKER!*"

ARSCHLOCH
N. GERMAN FOR "*ARSESWIPE!*"

SHARMUTA
N. ARABIC FOR "*BITCH*", USED TO REFER TO
A PERSON WHO SLEEPS WITH ANYONE.

FACIEM DURUM CACANTIS HABES

expr. Latin phrase meant as an insult to someone unattractive. It roughly translates to "*you have the face of a man with severe constipation*".

GET BENT

expr. Used to rudely dismiss someone, likely after they have said something that offends you or that greatly annoys you. Similar to telling someone to "*take a hike!*" or "*get lost!*"

TARFU
expr. Military slang for a perceived injustice. Stands for "*Totally And Royally Fucked Up*".

COME OFF IT
interj. Similar to "*you're kidding me!*" or "*no way!*"

COOTER
n. Female genitalia.

DRONGO
N. AUSTRALIAN WORD TO DESCRIBE A
DUMB PERSON. A FOOL OR A LOSER.

PUT A SOCK IN IT
EXPR. "*IT*" REFERS TO YOUR MOUTH. THIS IS
ANOTHER WAY TO SAY "*SHUT YOUR FACE!*"

CRAPCHUTE
N. A SITUATION IN WHICH EVERY
POSSIBLE OUTCOME IS TERRIBLE.

NUTSACK

INTERJ. SIMILAR TO "*DAMMIT!*", COMMONLY YELLED AFTER MAKING A MINOR MISTAKE OR EXPERIENCING PAIN SUCH AS STUBBING YOUR TOE, BUMPING YOUR ELBOW OR EVEN TAKING A BLOW TO YOUR PRIVATES.

GODDAMMIT DUDE PULL YOUR HEAD OUT OF YOUR ARSE

interj. Something a driver might say to himself out loud after missing the exit for the second time in a row. Used to say "*get with the programme*" or "*snap out of it*".

ARSE ABOUT
v. To putter, to waste time or behave in a stupid or childish manner.

NOOKIE
n. Slang for sexual intercourse.

NARK
n. A government paid spy. A rat or an informant.

YOU STUPID SHITE

interj. Something you might yell at someone who has done something disastrous or unfortunate, similar to "*you moron!*" but stronger.

Example:
Dan: "*Hey Vlad, the cake you left in the fridge was delicious; I ate it all up!*"
Vlad: "*That cake was the main dessert for tonight's big dinner, you stupid shite!*"

RAT-ARSED
ADJ. OLD ENGLISH TO DESCRIBE SOMEONE WHO IS SLOSHED. TO BE WASTED, DRUNK.

PANTY SNIFFER
N. SOMEONE WHO SMELLS WOMEN'S UNDERWEAR FOR PLEASURE. A PERVERT.

ARSE-SPICE
N. THE BURNING SENSATION AROUND YOUR BUMHOLE AFTER SHITTING OUT THE REMNANTS OF A VERY SPICY MEAL.

JUG SMUGGLER

n. An oversized bra used specifically for women whose boobs are so enormous they can't be contained by the standard sizes, requiring something a little more... tailored.

MOTOR-BOATING

v. The act of placing your face in between a woman's breasts, then making the sound of a boat's motor with your mouth while rapidly moving your face from one boob to the other.

MILF

n. Stands for *"Mum I'd Like to Fuck"*.

DILF

n. Stands for *"Dad I'd Like to Fuck"*.

TILF

n. Stands for *"Teacher I'd Like to Fuck"*.

TO DRAIN THE MAIN VEIN
EXPR. TO GO NUMBER ONE.
TO TINKLE. TO PEE.

PORTHOLE
N. ANOTHER WORD FOR ANUS, LIKELY
DUE TO ITS TIGHT ROUND SHAPE.

CHICKENSHIT
N. A WORTHLESS OR CONTEMPTIBLE
PERSON. SOMEONE WHO DOES
NOTHING RIGHT OR IS A COWARD.

GOING APESHIT

V. TO LOSE YOUR MIND OVER SOMETHING AND EXHIBIT PHYSICAL MANIFESTATIONS OF ANGER AND RAGE. TO LOSE CONTROL OF YOUR FEELINGS AND ACT LIKE AN INSANE PERSON. TO GO BANANAS, TO GO NUTS.

ARSE CLAP

n. When a person has a juicy or thick enough arse that they can manoeuvre and shake it in such a way that their cheeks come together to make a satisfying clapping sound. It is also a reference to the claps heard by solid sexual thrusts.

TO HALF-ARSE

v. To do something with minimal effort, usually below the minimum standards and with a complete lack of care.

MALÁKAS

n. Greek word for "*wanker*".

MOUSER

n. A woman's pubic-hair region.

SNOT ROCKET

n. A move that is best practised outside and involves placing your index finger firmly against one side of your nose to cut off one of your nasal cavities while you blow snot through the other, hard enough so that it shoots to the ground without the need for a tissue. Popular among athletes, especially those who do lots of field or distance running.

SHIT-FACED
N. TO BE SO DRUNK THAT YOUR FACE IS ALMOST UNRECOGNIZABLE. HAMMERED.

COCK ON CALL
N. A WOMAN'S SEX TOY.
BATTERIES INCLUDED.

TROUSER SNAKE
N. A GOOD-SIZED PENIS. NOT
TOO BIG, NOT TOO SMALL.

FRIDAY NIGHT BEAN-FLICKER

n. A woman who stays home Friday nights to pleasure herself and watch movies instead of wasting time going out in the hopes of getting drunk and laid.

BROWN EYE TO THE SKY

expr. A sexual position in which the receiver angles their back so that their face is in a pillow and their anus is up in the air for the taking.

TOSSER

n. A majorly obnoxious person. A jerkface.

TOOTS

n. An impolite way of saying "*babe*", or "*sweetie*". A broad. An attractive young woman.

QUIM TRIMMERS

n. A special set of clippers used specifically to trim a lady's bush.

THAT'S SO JIZZ
INTERJ. USED TO DESCRIBE SOMETHING
THAT IS SO EXCITING OR STIMULATING IT
COULD BE DESCRIBED AS ORGASMIC.

DICKWAD
N. ONE WHO IS SO DICKISH THAT
HE HAS THE DICKING ABILITIES
OF AN ENTIRE WAD OF DICKS.

ARSE FUDGE
N. THIS MEANS POOP, BUT IT CAN
ALSO BE USED TO TELL SOMEONE
THEY'VE DONE A CRAP JOB.

WHAT A TOOL

EXPR. SAY THIS WHILE POINTING AT A PERSON WHO IS EITHER SUGGESTING OR DOING SOMETHING INCREDIBLY FOOLISH. AN INSULT FOR SOMEONE WHO ISN'T BRIGHT AND HAS TOO MUCH TESTOSTERONE.

HOECAKE

n. In the southern states of the US this is a delicious dish similar to corn bread, but in other parts of the country it's an insult describing someone who lacks respect; a sucker.

NO ME CAGAS EL PALO
expr. "*Cagar*" means "*to shit*",
and "*palo*" means "*stick*".
Together, it's Mexican slang
for "*don't fuck with me*".

NO MAMES
expr. Similar to "*no fucking
way!*" in Spanish.

COMEMIERDA
n. Spanish for "*shithead*".

NO MORE FUCKS TO GIVE
expr. Describes when someone
has truly reached the end of their
capacity to care about others or bad
things happening in the world. To be
depleted of sympathy, compassion or
consideration, either for something
specific or life in general.

Example:
Jim: "*Janice, what are your thoughts
about the upcoming election?*"
Janice: "*Honestly, I'm feeling
pretty resigned to it all. I have
no more fucks to give.*"

HOLY MOSES
INTERJ. LIKE SAYING "*HOLY COW!*" OR "*GOOD LORD!*"

DAMN YOUR HIDE
EXPR. SAID TO SOMEONE YOU WISH TO CONDEMN OR DENOUNCE IN A MOMENT OF ANGER.

WHAT THE DEUCE?
EXPR. SWEAR ALTERNATIVE USED TO EXPRESS SHOCK. SIMILAR TO SAYING "*WHAT THE HELL!?*"

QUE PEDO?

expr. Literally translates to "*what fart?*" but used like "*what's up mate?*" Another variation in some parts of Mexico is "*¿que pedo trais buey?*", which is a combative way of asking "*what's your fucking problem?*"

TWO-BIT WHACK JOB

n. Someone who is not only lesser than but also does not conform to societal norms in a very outwardly apparent manner. A crazy person, like Joker from *Batman*.

MAMALUKE
n. A casual Italian-American insult for someone who is quite foolish or silly.

SCHMUCK
n. Yiddish for "*dick*" or "*jerkhead*".

KHNYOK
n. Yiddish word for a "*bigot*" or someone racist.

CUM DUMPSTER

N. SOMEONE GENDER NON-SPECIFIC WHO IS ONLY GOOD FOR OTHERS TO FINISH THEIR SEXUAL LOADS ONTO. COULD ALSO REFER TO SOMEONE WHO ACTUALLY ENJOYS BEING SHOWERED WITH JIZZ.

MEAT WHISTLE

n. Slang for penis. Used to describe someone who lacks the courage to do something. Someone who pretends to be tough but when faced with a real challenge, backs down.

PIPE DOWN
EXPR. A RUDE WAY OF SAYING
"*SIMMER DOWN!*" OR "*SHUT UP!*"

TROGLODYTE
N. AN INSULT FOR A PERSON WHO IS
SO AWFUL IT MAKES YOU QUESTION
WHY HUMANS HAVEN'T GONE EXTINCT
YET. A WASTE OF OXYGEN.

PROPER FUCKED
EXPR. THIS TERM IS USED TO DESCRIBE
SOMEONE BEING "*OFFED*" OR "*FULLY
TAKEN CARE OF*". TO BE MURDERED.

PISS-WIZARD

n. One who is masterful at consuming alcohol, capable of drinking large amounts while remaining fairly lucid. Someone who can hold their liquor.

UNFUCKWITHABLE

adj. The sensation of being on top of the world. When you are so much at peace with yourself that nothing anyone says or does can bring you down. Feeling impervious to negativity and drama.

TALLYWASHER
n. Someone who cleans penises with their mouth. A cocksucker.

LICKSPITTLE
n. An apple polisher, someone who is a suck-up. An arse-kisser.

TRIPPIN' BALLS
v. To be under the heavy influence of a drug, weed, or mushroom in a way that is immediately apparent to others due to the erratic or uncharacteristic mannerisms being exhibited.

COCKWOMBLE

N. A PERSON WHO BEHAVES INAPPROPRIATELY, IS USELESS AND OFTEN SPOUTS NONSENSE WHILE SIMULTANEOUSLY HOLDING A HIGH OPINION OF THEMSELF.

STUPID SONBITCH

expr. In the southern states of the US this is an artistic take on "*son of a bitch*". And not just any son of a bitch, but one who is annoyingly unintelligent to boot.

WAZZOCK
n. A very dumb or annoying person.

GIT
n. Someone stupid, a moron.

STFU
expr. Stands for "*Shut The Fuck Up!*"

JESUS H. CHRIST ALMIGHTY
INTERJ. USED TO EXPRESS SHOCK OR
UNCONTROLLABLE FRUSTRATION.

FECK
INTERJ. IN IRELAND, THIS IS USED TO
EXPRESS ANNOYANCE OR FRUSTRATION.

HOLY JUMPING JESUS
EXPR. LIKE SAYING *"GOOD GOD!"*
OR *"BLOODY HELL!"*

QUACK

n. A snake-oil salesman, someone who sells bogus goods, medicines or potions to foolish buyers who are easily enamoured by myths and ancient tales.

ARSEMONKEY

n. An individual who habitually and quickly messes up situations that would otherwise require a decent amount of time, effort, or patience to see through correctly. A big screw-up.

STUNAD
n. Italian-American slang for a
"*stupid person*". Comes from the
Italian word "*stonato*", which means
"*out of tune*" or "*tone-deaf*".

VA CREVER
expr. French for "*I hope you die!*"

MERDE
n./expr. Means "*shit*" in French
but is also used as a common
way of saying "*good luck!*"

TO PUT YOUR ARSE
ON THE LINE

v. To put yourself in a vulnerable
position for the sake of someone
else, often with the risk of being
negatively impacted by the
outcome. This phrase is often used
by businessmen who are in the
middle of negotiating a big deal.

Example:

*"I'm putting my arse on the line
for you Tom; you better bring
your A-game and be prepared
to impress this client."*

DIE KACKE IST AM DAMPFEN
N. GERMAN PHRASE THAT MEANS THINGS ARE
ESCALATING, GETTING WORSE. TRANSLATES
TO *"THE SHIT'S HITTING THE FAN!"*

FICKGESICHT
N. "FUCKFACE!" IN GERMAN.

STINKSTIEFEL
N. IN GERMAN, THIS IS A MISERABLE OR RUDE
PERSON, SIMILAR TO *"GIT"* (SEE PAGE 68).

FIGMO

EXPR. MILITARY SLANG THAT STANDS FOR *"FUCK IT GOT MY ORDERS"*. IN OTHER WORDS, THERE'S NOTHING ELSE THAT CAN BE DONE TO STOP WHATEVER SITUATION IS PLAYING OUT. LIKE SAYING *"MY HANDS ARE TIED"*.

DON'T LET IT HIT YA WHERE THE GOOD LORD SPLIT YA

expr. A rude way of telling someone to leave, to *"get the hell out!"*. The *"split"* references your butt crack. In other words, *"don't let the door hit your arse on your way out!"*

BUTT-BREATH

n. Used either to describe someone's heinous breath or as an insult to someone who is very annoying or unpleasant. An arse.

TO BE HALF RATS

expr. Old English. To be partially drunk. A little tipsy. To have a good buzz going.

DUMBASS

n. A stupid person, either by lacking common knowledge or engaging in foolish behaviour.

SHNOOKER-DOOKIES
INTERJ. USED TO EXPRESS SURPRISE,
SIMILAR TO "*HOLY CRAP!*"

BED-SWERVER
N. SOMEONE WHO GOES FROM ONE BED
TO ANOTHER TO HAVE SEX. A CHEATER.

HANKY-PANKY
N. SEXUAL BEHAVIOUR, OFTEN THE
KIND THAT IS IMPROPER FOR THAT
SETTING OR CIRCUMSTANCE.

DON'T GET ALL AGGRO

expr. Something you might say with a raised voice to someone who is becoming angry or on the verge of carrying out an unwarranted microaggression. A snarky way of telling someone to "*chill out!*"

TO KNOCK UP

v. To get a woman pregnant, usually without the intention of actually wanting to have a baby. This inevitably puts both people in a difficult position, forcing an uncomfortable but necessary conversation about how to proceed.

CABRÃO
n. Means "*bastard*" or
"*fucker*" in Portuguese.

CHUPA-MOS
expr. Portuguese for "*suck 'em*".

REGO DO CU
n. Means "*arse crack*" in Portuguese.

TO MAKE A TIT OF YOURSELF

expr. To make a fool of yourself. To do something embarrassing or idiotic in plain view, where several people can see and judge you negatively for it.

Example:

"Did Rene do some heavy drinking on her lunch break? She's making a tit of herself dancing like that in front of our overseas clients."

VAJAYJAY
N. A WOMAN'S GENITALS.

GENTLEMAN'S RELISH
N. BRITISH BRAND OF ANCHOVY PASTE.
IT IS ALSO SLANG FOR EJACULATE.

MUCKENDER
N. A CONVENIENT RAG THAT ONE CARRIES
WITH THEM TO REMOVE UNWANTED MUCK OR
SCHMUTZ. A HANDKERCHIEF. A SNOT RAG.

ADIOS MOTHERFUCKER

N. A HARD-HITTING LIGHT BLUE COCKTAIL MADE WITH VODKA, RUM, TEQUILA, GIN, BLUE CURAÇAO, 7UP, SWEET & SOUR, AND A CITRUS GARNISH. NAMED AFTER THE SPANISH WORD "*ADIOS*", MEANING "*GOODBYE*" BECAUSE IT'LL PUT YOU ON YOUR ARSE.

COCK-BLOCK

v. The intentional act of preventing someone from engaging in a sexual conquest. It can also be used as a noun, describing a person who regularly interferes with others while they are flirting and trying to hook up.

ÁDE GAMÍSOU
expr. Greek for "*fuck you!*"

HÉSTIKA
expr. Greek phrase that translates
as "*I don't give a shit!*"

KARIÓLIS
n. Greek word for "*douche*".
Considered very offensive.

HOLY GUACAMOLE

expr. A nice innocent avocado-based oath expressing astonishment or enthusiasm, suitable for use by vegans.

DICKSICLE

n. When a male wants to have sex, finds himself in a situation with a ready and willing partner, but it's much too cold for him to get an erection... he's got a dicksicle on his hands.

CHEESED OFF
ADJ. TICKED OFF, PEEVED,
HIGHLY ANNOYED.

BUM AROUND
V. TO BE LAZY, IDLE, OR
FRUSTRATINGLY UNPRODUCTIVE.

KNACKERED
ADJ. DESCRIBES THE WAY YOU MIGHT
FEEL THE MORNING AFTER A LONG
NIGHT OF DRINKING. WORN OUT.

HELLA

ADV. CALIFORNIAN SLANG THAT WAS POPULARIZED IN THE LATE 90s AND EARLY 2000s. A COOL KIDS' SUBSTITUTE FOR *"VERY"* OR *"LOTS"*.

FAIR SUCK OF THE SAUCE BOTTLE

expr. In Australia, this phrase is used to ask or demand that justice be served, that whatever is being requested is a reasonable ask.

GET STUFFED
expr. "*Get lost!*" or "*Piss off!*"

GANNET
n. An avaricious person,
a greedy bastard.

GOSH DARNIT
interj. Mild form of "*goddammit!*",
commonly used in the southern US.

BLESS YOUR HEART

expr. In the US, this seemingly kind phrase is used in some parts of the country as a way of expressing genuine sympathy or admiration of someone's good will. However, in most of the southern states, it is actually a backhanded phrase of condescension used as an insult. What they're really saying is "*poor bastard*" or "*what an idiot*".

FLEABAG
N. A LIVING CREATURE THAT ATTRACTS MANY FLEAS BUT USED TO RUDELY DESCRIBE A PERSON OR ANIMAL THAT IS VERY DIRTY.

PUCKERHOLE
N. THE EXIT OF YOUR POOP CHUTE. YOUR ANUS.

BEAVER
N. A WOMAN'S LADY PARTS. HER VULVA.

TO GET YOUR KNICKERS IN A TWIST

expr. To get worked up or upset over something that isn't that big of a deal. Often employed in the negative.

FUCK THAT NOISE

expr. Used to vehemently dismiss an idea, situation or proposition.

ASS-HAT
n. A stupid or contemptible person, a jackass.

TODGER
n. Another word for "*penis*" in the UK, Australia, Canada and New Zealand.

BITCHIN'
interj. A cool way to express excitement or enthusiasm for something. Similar to "*sweet!*"

SHWING

INTERJ. AN EXCLAMATION OF SEXUAL EXCITEMENT BY A MALE WHEN LAYING EYES ON AN ATTRACTIVE WOMAN. INTENDED TO MIMIC THE NOISE OF A SWORD BEING UNSHEATHED. THE METAPHORICAL SOUND OF SOMEONE GETTING A QUICK ERECTION.

A BUNCH OF FUCKERY

expr. A stronger alternative to "*bullshit!*" Can also be used to describe deceitful actions, nonsensical/over-the-top behaviour or an injustice.

ARSE GOBLIN
N. SOMEONE YOU DON'T LIKE,
A BIT OF A JERK-OFF.

TO SCUMBER
V. TO VOID YOUR BOWELS,
TO DEFECATE.

DICK-TAC
N. A CUTE LITTLE PENIS. ALSO, A TINY
PENIS ENTERING THE MOUTH DURING
ORAL SEX, RESEMBLING THE FAMOUS
MINT KNOWN AS A TIC-TAC.

BLIMEY
interj. Used to express astonishment at something or someone's actions or words. Popular in the UK.

BITCH PLEASE
expr. Used to question the validity of something someone says. To challenge them with conviction.

GOBSHITE

n. One who engages in useless chatter or unwanted small talk. A loud-mouthed moron.

BAG OF DICKS

n. Someone who is so much of a jerk they exceed the average level of dickishness.

SCROTE

n. Someone who is so insignificant and useless that they don't even deserve the second syllable of the full insult; "*scrotum*".

BLOW IT OUT YOUR ARSE
expr. Used to aggressively
dismiss or deflect unwanted
commentary by others.

Example:
Jim: "*Bob, you look terrible. Did
you have a rough night with the
ladies or is this a new look?*"
Bob: "*Blow it out your arse, Jim.*"

SHITKICKER
N. AN UNSOPHISTICATED OR OAFISH PERSON, USUALLY FROM A VERY RURAL AREA THAT TRAVELLERS ARE UNLIKELY TO VISIT.

SNOWFLAKE
N. OVERLY EMOTIONAL AND EASILY OFFENDED PERSON WHO IS OFTEN UNABLE TO COPE WITH ANY FORM OF OPPOSITION. A SOFTY.

SHITASTROPHE
N. USED TO DESCRIBE A HUGE MISTAKE THAT CANNOT BE SALVAGED. SOMETHING WORSE THAN A CATASTROPHE.

COÛTER LA PEAU DES FESSES

EXPR. FRENCH PHRASE THAT MEANS SOMETHING IS INCREDIBLY PRICEY, NEARLY TO THE POINT OF BEING UNAFFORDABLE. IT LITERALLY TRANSLATES TO *"COSTS THE SKIN OFF YOUR ARSE"*, THE EQUIVALENT OF *"COSTS AN ARM AND A LEG"*.

PORCA PUTTANA

expr. In Italian *"porca"* means pig and *"puttana"* means prostitute. This commonly used expression is for displaying shock in a vulgar manner, like exclaiming *"fucking hell!"*

CONNARD
n. French for "*bastard*",
"*jerk*", or "*arsehole*".

JE M'EN FOUS
expr. French phrase meaning
"*I don't give a fuck!*"

VA TE FAIRE FOUTRE
expr. French for "*go fuck yourself!*"

FERSCHNICKET
ADJ. IN YIDDISH, IT MEANS TO BE
"DRUNK OFF YOUR ARSE".

TUCHES
N. YIDDISH FOR *"BUTTOCKS"*. A WORD
AN ANGRY MUM MIGHT USE TOWARDS
HER SON: *"GET OFF YOUR TUCHES!"*

SHMENDRICK
N. IN YIDDISH, THIS TERM IS GENERALLY
USED TO BELITTLE SOMEONE WHO IS WEAK
OR PHYSICALLY NON-THREATENING.

BOHICA

expr. Military slang indicating something bad is about to happen; stands for "*Bend Over Here It Comes Again*", indicating that the group is about to take it up the rear (metaphorically).

COJONES

n. Spanish for "*balls*". Generally used to describe someone with courage or grit.

COCKBURGER
n. Someone who is incredibly arrogant or pedantic.

FURBURGER
n. An unshaved vulva.

BURGASM
n. The feeling of intense pleasure when you take that first mouth-watering bite of a deliciously juicy hamburger, especially after a super long wait while being incredibly hungry.

STINK EYE

n. Another word for anus. It also refers to the look in someone's eyes when they stare you down in a questionable or suspicious manner.

Example:
"*That guy at the register must have thought I was going to steal something; he was giving me stink eye the entire time I was in the store.*"

BUZZ OFF
EXPR. WHEN SOMEONE IS ANNOYING YOU, TELL THEM TO *"BUZZ OFF!"* MEANING *"GO AWAY!"*

SHOVE IT
EXPR. USED TO RUDELY DISMISS SOMEONE. SHORT FOR *"SHOVE IT UP YOUR ARSE!"*

TO WEASEL-DICK
V. AN EXPRESSION USED TO DESCRIBE WHEN SOMEONE TRIES TO SNEAK THEIR WAY INTO OR OUT OF SOMETHING, BUT IN A VERY SHADY OR MORALLY QUESTIONABLE MANNER.

COCK-UP
N./V. A MISTAKE OR TO SCREW-UP.

YOUR MOUTH'S WRITING CHECKS THAT YOUR ASS CAN'T CASH

expr. US expression said to someone when they are running their mouth about something that they can't back up or substantiate, either with their actual body, their skills or any other form of corroboration.

EDE FAECUM
expr. Latin for "*eat shit!*"

PODEX PERFECTUS ES
expr. Latin phrase meaning
"*you're a complete arsehole*".

FUTUTUS ET MORI IN IGNI
expr. Latin for "*fuck off
and die in a fire*".

FOR CRYIN' OUT LOUD
INTERJ. POLITE WAY OF EXCLAIMING
"FOR CHRIST'S SAKE!"

SON OF A MOTHERLESS GOAT
INTERJ. MILD VERSION OF
"SON OF A BITCH!"

CRUD MUFFIN
INTERJ. TAMER VERSION OF *"SHIT!"*,
USUALLY USED BY SOMEONE WHO IS
DISAPPOINTED OR AT A LOSS FOR WORDS.

POCKET POOL

n. When a man reaches into his side pocket to scratch an itch on his genitals with his index finger, similar to the way a game of billiards is played (with sticks poking balls).

BONERIFIC

interj. An enthusiastic reply to something that sounds great to you. It is similar to exclaiming "*fantastic!*" or "*fabulous!*"

Example:

Matt: "*How does pizza sound for tonight?*"
Jake: "*Bonerific!*"

SPOOGE
n. That silky white love juice that comes from a happy penis. Cockspit.

BOGGARD
n. Old English for "*a toilet*".

TO BE HARD-BAKED
expr. When you are unable to dump your load because it simply won't come out, no matter how hard you push. Old English for "*constipation*".

TO DICK SOMEONE AROUND
v. To intentionally mess with someone's head, waste their time or mislead them in a harsh or unfair manner.

Example:
"I think it's time you look for another job; your boss is just dicking you around and has no intention of giving you the promotion he promised."

QUALEM MULEIRCULAM
EXPR. LATIN FOR *"WHAT A BIMBO!"*

PUTA QUE PARIU
INTERJ. MEANS *"HOLY SHIT!"*
IN PORTUGUESE.

VACA
N. PORTUGUESE FOR *"COW"*.

SUCK IT/SUCK ON THAT
EXPR. USED PRIMARILY AS A WAY OF CLAIMING A MINOR VICTORY OR TRIUMPH, BUT ALSO AS AN EMPHATIC ENDING TO SOMETHING. COULD ALSO BE USED AS A TAUNT OR PUT-DOWN.

TO HAVE THE SQUITS
expr. To have a bad case of diarrhoea.

VERPISS DICH
expr. German for "*get lost!*" or "*piss off!*"

DU BLÖDE KUH
expr. German insult meaning "*you stupid cow*".

DEINE MUTTER SÄUGT SCHWEINE
expr. German phrase meaning "*your mother suckles pigs!*"

CHRIST ON A CRACKER
INTERJ. AN EXPRESSION USED TO CONVEY SHOCK OR FRUSTRATION, SIMILAR TO "*BLOODY HELL!*"

HORSE-SHIT
N. SIMILAR TO "*BULLSHIT*" BUT HAS MORE OF A NONSENSICAL OR RUBBISH CONNOTATION RATHER THAN ONE OF DECEPTION.

BUGGER
N. QUITE A VERSATILE WORD. IT COULD REFER TO A RASCAL OR WORTHLESS PERSON, OR BE USED AS AN INTERJECTION, SIMILAR TO "*DAMN!*"

TO WORK SOMEONE'S ARSE OFF

expr. A rude phrase meaning to make someone work incredibly hard, so much so that their arse actually begins to disappear from the energy being expended.

YOU BET YOUR SWEET ARSE

expr. Could be used as a threat or to confirm something in an enthusiastic manner.

Example:

Julius: "*Hey Jenny, are you going to be at my graduation tomorrow?*"
Jenny: "*You bet your sweet arse I am!*"

KUTTAAR BAACHA
expr. Bengali phrase meaning "*son of a dog!*" or "*son of a bitch!*"

BOKA CHODA
n. Bengali for "*dumbfuck*".

BUND
n. Punjabi for "*arse*".

THE MORE YOU STIR THE SHIT THE MORE IT STINKS

expr. Meaning the more you mess with an unpleasant situation, the more likely it is to worsen. If someone is known for engaging in this behaviour regularly, they are called a "*shit-stirrer.*"

Example:
"*Look at Ryan over there trying to get Louise to say something bad about her husband in front of her boss. He is such a shit-stirrer!*"

TO MEERKAT
EXPR. TO GET A QUICK AND UNEXPECTED ERECTION, SIMILAR TO THE BODY LANGUAGE OF A MEERKAT WHEN IT STANDS UP STRAIGHT.

RELATIONSHIT
N. A POOR OR UNHEALTHY RELATIONSHIP BETWEEN TWO PEOPLE, ONE THAT INEVITABLY ENDS ON VERY BAD TERMS.

STUPITCH
N. A GENDER NON-SPECIFIC STUPID BITCH. SOMEONE WHO IS BOTH HIGHLY UNPLEASANT *AND* IDIOTIC.

SHUT THAT SHIT DOWN
EXPR. TO PUT AN IMMEDIATE STOP
TO SOMETHING QUESTIONABLE
OR WRONG.

WHOOPTY FUCKIN' DOO!
expr. Used sarcastically to
express disingenuous enthusiasm
for someone or something.

SWAMP ARSE

n. A sweaty wetness in the butt crack that usually soaks through one's underwear.

ARSE-WIPE

n. An annoying or useless person.

DIPSHIT

n. Someone who is inept, dumb.

GTFOH

expr. Stands for "*Get The Fuck Outta Here*". An interjection that is used either literally to tell someone to leave or metaphorically, similar to "*get outta town!*" or "*you're kidding me, right?*"

SNAFU

expr. Believed to have originated in the military, this is now a fairly common term short for "*Situation Normal All Fucked Up*", used to describe a problem or escalation in an otherwise ordinary circumstance.

QUE TE PICA
EXPR. SPANISH PHRASE THAT TRANSLATES TO
"WHAT'S GOT YOUR KNICKERS IN A TWIST?",
SIMILAR TO *"WHAT'S YOUR PROBLEM?"*

PINCHE
ADV. SPANISH WORD FOR A "KITCHEN
BOY"; LOW-LEVEL HELPER. ALSO USED
AS AN ADVERB TO ENHANCE ADJECTIVES
LIKE *"THIS FUCKING GUY!"*

VALE MADRE
EXPR. A WAY OF SAYING *"I DON'T
GIVE A SHIT"* IN SPANISH SLANG.

RING-PIECE OPERA

n. A prolonged series of loud farts at different tones and pitches, especially when heard from another room or across the hallway, like in a theatre.

Example:

"Jesus, after that ring-piece opera I suggest you take a trip to the restroom and do a trouser check."

SHITSHOW
n. A very hectic and disorganized situation. A chaotic scene that is getting out of hand.

FUCKBOY
n. A male who not only has careless sex with multiple partners in short periods of time, but often gives mixed signals. Someone who shouldn't be taken seriously or trusted.

TO BITCH-SLAP
v. To publicly slap someone across their face to humiliate them, usually because they did something to deserve it.

PROCRASTURBATING

v. To procrastinate with accomplishing a pressing or important task by stopping to take a masturbation break. This could also refer to holding off achieving climax in the hopes of experiencing greater pleasure once you finally do finish.

BEEF BAYONET

N. A SHOCKINGLY LARGE PENIS THAT IS BOTH IMPRESSIVE AND SLIGHTLY FRIGHTENING. THE KIND YOU MIGHT COME ACROSS IN AN ADULT VIDEO.

THE SHIT
ADJ. SOMETHING OR SOMEONE THAT
IS EXCEPTIONAL OR TOP-NOTCH.

THE SHITTER
N. THE JOHN. THE CRAP CASTLE.
THE TOILET.

TO BE IN DEEP SHIT
EXPR. TO BE IN SERIOUS
TROUBLE OR DANGER.

JESUS, MARY AND JOSEPH!

interj. Used to express major
astonishment or profound
frustration, more than
just saying "*Jesus!*"

TO HELL WITH THIS

expr. Used to convey a sense
of hopelessness or resignation
from a situation that you have
decided you are now done with.

HOLY FRIJOLES

interj. "*Frijoles*" is Spanish for
beans. Similar to saying "*holy
cow!*" or "*holy smokes!*"

BY THE BEARD OF ZEUS
interj. Exclamation of surprise, to be impressed by something or someone.

COME HELL OR HIGH WATER
expr. Whatever difficulties may occur, you will succeed in accomplishing the task at hand. Similar to saying "*no matter what*".

TO LOSE YOUR SHIT

expr. Describes a situation of anger that gets way out of your control. When you become completely unglued. To become enraged.

Example:
"Kevin lost his shit when he realized that his favourite employee had been stealing from the company for months. He fired him on the spot and had security escort him off the premises."

SOD IT
EXPR. USED AS A STRONG EXCLAMATION OF ANNOYANCE OR DISREGARD; "*SCREW IT!*" ALSO CONSIDER "*SOD OFF!*", MEANING "*BEAT IT!*"

MUNTER
N. AN UGLY PERSON.

FUGLY
ADJ. DESCRIBING A PERSON, PLACE OR THING THAT IS "*FUCKING UGLY*".

BITCH ARSE
N. SOMEONE WHO'S ALL BARK AND NO BITE, WHO ACTS TOUGH UNTIL CHALLENGED BY SOMEONE, ONLY TO BACK DOWN LIKE A WIMP. AN OVER-COMPENSATOR.

TWAT-WAFFLE
n. An imbecile who wields his stupidity as a weapon in order to gain positions of power and engage in corruption, often harmful to others.

CHOOCH
n. Italian-American slang for
a meathead, stupid person.

ARRECHO
adj./n. Spanish word. Depending
on the geographical region,
can mean "*horny*", describe
someone who is furious, or refer
to someone who is a nuisance.

MOMZER
n. In Yiddish, this term is used to
describe a "*shady*" or "*untrustworthy
person*". A snake to watch out for.

TO BUST SOMEONE'S BALLS

expr. To give someone a hard time,
to tease or joke with someone.

Example:

*"Seth likes to bust balls at work,
but he's harmless. He doesn't mean
any offence by it, don't worry."*

TO NOT GIVE TWO
SHITS ABOUT

expr. To suggest you really
don't care about something.

Example:

*"I don't give two shits about
Tim's commitment issues, that's
not my problem to solve!"*

VESCERE BRACIS MEIS
EXPR. LATIN INSULT MEANING
"EAT MY SHORTS".

ASCENDO TUUM
EXPR. MEANS *"UP YOURS"* IN LATIN.

ES MUNDUS EXCREMENTI
EXPR. LATIN PHRASE THAT TRANSLATES
TO *"YOU ARE A PILE OF SHIT"*.

AT THE ARSE CRACK OF DAWN

N. EXTREMELY EARLY IN THE MORNING. AT OR EVEN BEFORE DAYBREAK, OFTEN USED WITH A REGRETTABLE OR LAMENTABLE TONE.

FUCK KNUCKLE

interj. Something you shout when you're in a wee bit of trouble.

Example:
"Oh, fuck knuckle! I left the hose running all night long!"

HELLISH

adj. Used to describe something unpleasant, awful or nightmarish.

PRICK

n. Another one of dozens of words for penis. Also, a dude who's kind of an arsehole.

COLD BASTARD

n. A heartless person who has no compassion or capacity to empathize with other people's emotions or even begin to understand their struggles.

TO TAKE THE PISS OUT OF

expr. To make fun of someone or mock them, but to their face and in a light-hearted manner, not behind their back. To have a laugh at someone else's expense.

Example:

Harry: *"Mate, you still owe me money from last night's bet, remember?"*

Tom: *"What are you talking about?"*

Harry: *"Last night! You bet me you could drink more than me, but you passed out before you could even finish your fourth pint. You owe me 40 quid!"*

Tom: *"You taking the piss out of me or what!?"*

ICH WÜRDE MICH LIEBER INS KNIE FICKEN

expr. A fantastic German phrase used to convey strong opposition to a proposition or idea. It translates as "*I'd rather go fuck myself!*"

AMBITCHOUS

adj. Describes one's unwavering desire to be most unpleasant. Striving, somehow, to be more of a bitch than the average bitch. An overly ambitious bitch.

HORSE PUCKY
INTERJ. SOFTER VERSION OF
"HORSE-SHIT!" (SEE PAGE 113)

DOG SHIT
ADJ. TO BE UNIQUELY UNSKILLED,
TO SUCK BADLY AT SOMETHING.

BULL SPIT
INTERJ. A LESS OFFENSIVE WAY OF
CHALLENGING SOMEONE'S CLAIM.
LIKE *"BS!"* OR *"NONSENSE!"*

ARSCHGESICHT

n. German for "*arseface*".

CHE PALLE

expr. Although "*palle*" is Italian
for balls, this phrase means
"*what a pain in the arse!*"

MINCHIA

interj. Italian, used to express
surprise, anger or disappointment.
Translates to "*fuck!*"

FUCK AROUND AND FIND OUT
expr. A taunt or dare directed at an individual or group who has committed to an action or course that is likely to have negative consequences. It can also describe one's incredibly reckless behaviour.

Example:
Bianca: "*I thought we told Fabien not to push his luck driving without a permit late at night from downtown.*"
Elizabeth: "*Yes, we did, but Fabien is a real fuck-around-and-find-out kind of guy – I don't think he exercises much caution in his day-to-day life.*"

SHIT FOR BRAINS
N. DESCRIBES SOMEONE WHO FALLS FOR SILLY TRICKS OR IS EASILY FOOLED. SOMEONE WHO REPEATEDLY MAKES BAD MISTAKES AND HAS A VERY LIMITED CAPACITY FOR REASONING. A BUFFOON. A COMPLETE IDIOT.

LIKE I GIVE A SHIT
expr. Sarcastic expression that you might use when you're feeling particularly sassy and you aren't really invested in what someone is saying. Another variation is "ask me if I give a shit."

GAYEE DE
EXPR. IN ORIYA, SPOKEN IN PARTS OF
INDIA, THIS MEANS *"FUCK OFF!"*

RUPFU TSUNG
EXPR. INSULT FROM THE LOTHA NAGA
LANGUAGE OF INDIA, WHICH TRANSLATES
TO *"CYST IN THE RECTUM"*.

CHATANA BANDHAR GADHA
EXPR. INDIAN SWEAR PHRASE
MEANING *"LICK MONKEY ARSE"*.

DORK
n. An idiot, a loser. Someone with limited social skills.

SCUMBAG
n. Someone who is engaged in dishonest or unethical behaviour for personal gain.

KNOCKERS
n. A nice pair of hooters. Fun-sized breasts.

CLUSTERFUCK

n. A situation that is either out of control or rapidly worsening, often with an element of panic or chaos and involving many people.

Example:
"Don't go to shopping centres during the week between Christmas and New Year; it's an absolute clusterfuck out there!"

SHUT THE FRONT DOOR

expr. A less offensive way of asking someone to shut up. Can also be used like "*you're kidding me!*"

Example:
Joanna: "*I won $1000 gambling in Las Vegas!*"
Joanna's mum: "*Shut the front door! Really?*"

JUST FUCKING PEACHY

expr. A snarky and sarcastic reply to someone when they ask you how you're doing after you've had a crap day. Where "*peachy*" means great, this phrase means the opposite.

UN PUTERO
EXPR. IN SPANISH, IT IS USED TO DESCRIBE A LARGE AMOUNT OF SOMETHING. "*A FUCK TON OF...*"

FEH
INTERJ. IN YIDDISH, THIS IS USED TO DISPLAY DISGUST, DISAPPOINTMENT OR DISAPPROVAL OF SOMETHING.

SHUCKS
INTERJ. LIKE SAYING "*SHOOT!*" OR "*FUDGE!*" IN A MOMENT OF ANGER OR EMBARRASSMENT. IT IS ALSO USED AS AN EXPRESSION OF THANKS OR BASHFULNESS.

BLUE BALLS

n. Slang for the scientific term *"epididymal hypertension"*, a painful phenomenon that occurs in the testicles when a male is sexually aroused for an extended period of time but is never able to blow his load. This leads to a feeling of soreness in the sack that can last for hours.

BUTT-MUNCH

n. An insult for someone with a disagreeable personality, someone who you don't like.

TURD-SUCKER

n. Someone who either smokes cigars with style or is unattractive. Can also be used for someone who just sucks at life.

BADASS MOTHERFUCKER

n. The opposite of a turd-sucker, someone who is an allaround cool, tough and courageous person. Someone you might idolize for their swagger and cool vibes.

STREWTH

INTERJ. IN AUSTRALIA THIS TERM IS USED IN THE SAME VEIN AS "*HOLY SHIT!*" OR "*JESUS!*" WHAT YOU MIGHT SAY TO DESCRIBE YOUR THOUGHTS OR FEELINGS AFTER A LONG NIGHT OF DRINKING.

DERRO

n. Short for "*derelict*" in Australia, this refers to someone who just can't get their act together. Someone lazy or inept. A loose canon of sorts.

AIRY-FAIRY
ADJ. TO HAVE OVERLY WISHFUL
THINKING. TO BE IDEALISTIC IN A
FOOLISH WAY; IMPRACTICAL.

GORMLESS
ADJ. LACKING INITIATIVE, SHORT ON REASON.
SOMEONE WHO DOESN'T HAVE GOOD SENSE.

MALARKEY
N. NONSENSE TALK, JIBBER-JABBER.
A BUNCH OF MUMBO JUMBO.

CORNHOLE

n. The bunghole, the end of the dookie pipe. It is also a fun game where you stand at a distance and toss sandbags onto raised sheets of wood with a hole near the centre. The objective is to get the bag to land on the board or go through the hole, which yields three points.

TO GET SOME PUNANI
expr. "*To get laid*", usually used by males having guy talk or who are out on the prowl.

KOL KHARA
expr. In Arabic, this means "*eat shit!*"

CRIKEY
interj. A swear popularized by Steve Irwin, the crocodile-hunter. Used to express shock, like "*Christ!*"

BOGAN

n. In Australia, this refers to someone who is a bit rough around the edges. Someone unsophisticated who has trouble fitting in. A simpleton.

WRISTY

n. In Australia, this is a word to describe the act of pleasuring someone with your hand. Their version of a "*handjob*".

CRIMINY

INTERJ. SIMILAR TO SAYING *"OH COME ON!"* OR *"GIMME A BREAK!"*

BARMY

ADJ. STUPID OR CRAZY. GONE MAD.

PLONKER

N. AN IDIOT, SOMEONE RATHER STUPID.

SHITCANNED
v. TO BE FIRED. TO BE TERMINATED FROM YOUR PLACE OF WORK, USUALLY BECAUSE OF SOMETHING YOU DID THAT WAS WRONG OR UNETHICAL.

FUCKNUGGET
n. An insult to lob at someone who is incredibly disagreeable or menacingly idiotic.

LIMP-DICK

n. An ideal insult for someone who lacks substance or bravery. Someone weak, both physically and mentally. A pushover.

DICK-SNEEZE

n. A male orgasm.

TEABAGGING

v. When a male grips his shaft in his hand, tilting it upwards, squats over someone's open mouth and lowers himself to gently dip his nuts in and out.

HAM-BAGS

n. Old English for "a lady's undergarments". It can also refer to the female version of the sexual manoeuvre known as "*teabagging*".

FOR FUCK'S SAKE

expr. One of the more aggressive interjections, similar to saying "*oh come on!*" or "*what the hell!?*"

Example:

After a hot shower, Darlene's husband Paul sometimes forgets to bring a towel with him. Unfortunately, their bedroom is across the house from the bathroom and tonight Darlene has friends over for cocktails when she sees her husband walking through the kitchen naked...

Darlene: "*Paul, we have guests! For fuck's sake put some goddamn clothes on!*"

TO FUCK

v. To engage in a sexual act in which some form of penetration is achieved, usually vaginal or anal. Although it is commonly associated with the thrusts of a male, it is gender non-specific and can be used for both males and females alike.

SHIT-MAGNET

n. One who regularly attracts shitty or unfortunate circumstances. Someone who always finds themselves in some sort of trouble.

Have you enjoyed this book?

If so, find us on Facebook at
Summersdale Publishers, on
Twitter at **@Summersdale** and on
Instagram and TikTok at
@summersdalebooks
and get in touch.
We'd love to hear from you!

www.summersdale.com